50 THINGS TO KNOW ABOUT BIRDS IN COLORADO

Birding the Centennial State

Megan Miller

CZYK Publishing Since 2011.
CZYKPublishing.com
50 Things to Know

Lock Haven, PA
All rights reserved.
ISBN: 9798490324751

50 THINGS TO KNOW ABOUT BIRDS IN THE USA

If you know someone who loves birds, I cannot imagine them not learning or enjoying this book.

This book is perfect for both experienced birders and beginners alike. It is written in readable prose and studded with personal stories from the author's many years of observing birds.

50 Things to Know About Birds in Pennsylvania: Birding in the Keystone State
Author Darryl & Jackie Speicher

I really enjoyed this book. I live in the Badger state and I learned a lot of things I didn't know before. The author got me excited about taking up bird watching. Definitely going to plan a day trip to Horicon Marsh.

50 Things to Know About Birds in Wisconsin : Birding in the Badger State
Author Carly Lincoln

50 THINGS TO KNOW ABOUT BIRDS IN COLORADO

BOOK DESCRIPTION

Colorado is a state with breathtaking landscapes from the lowest prairies to the highest mountains. Its enormous diversity of habitats provides for an even larger diversity of plant, avian, and animal species. Its position in the center of the United States aligns with the central flyway, a major migratory path for all migrating birds. In addition, its overlap with the great plains means many eastern species can be found within the state's lines. A stop in Denver during migration can bring you eastern warblers as well as western species like Black-billed Magpie and Lazuli Bunting.

50 Things to Know about the Birds in Colorado offers an informative approach to finding a variety of birds across a variety of habitats. This book is broken down by season and habitat. Each habitat has descriptions including a brief breakdown of the plant community, elevation, and includes two short species profiles and one story about resident birds in that habitat. Colorado has extraordinary geography, & visiting any of these places during any season guarantees wonderful views and many opportunities to view wildlife during all times of the year.

TABLE OF CONTENTS

ABOUT THE AUTHOR

Megan is a lifelong birder and Ornithologist based out of Denver, Colorado. She started birding in elementary school with her local Audubon Society and never stopped. Her love of birds led her to complete a Fish, Conservation, and Wildlife Biology degree at Colorado State University where she served as the co-founder of CSU's first bird watching club. During and after college she has worked a variety of field jobs around the country including in North Dakota, Utah, Colorado, and Massachusetts. She aspires to work at a field museum or biological field station as a full-time researcher or science coordinator.

INTRODUCTION

*We shall never achieve harmony with the land,
anymore than we shall achieve absolute justice or
liberty for people. In these higher aspirations the
important thing is not to achieve but to strive.*

**— Aldo Leopold, Round River: From the Journals of Aldo
Leopold**

*My favorite quote: The land ethic simply
enlarges the boundaries of the community to
include soils, waters, plants, and animals, or
collectively: the land... In short, a land ethic
changes the role of Homo sapiens from conqueror
of the land-community to plain member and citizen
of it. It implies respect for his fellow-members, and
also respect for the community as such.*

— Aldo Leopold

This guide begins with a general introduction of seasonal birding
in Colorado and moves on briefly describing some of Colorado's
major habitats, their plant and birdlife, and locations where you can
find that habitat. I decided to include habitat descriptions because I
believe it's important to understand birds in the context of the land
they inhabit. Nothing is more important to education than

understanding the connections between birds, plants, animals, and the habitat's non biotic elements. Each element is a material and tool that builds and shapes the habitat until it stands in a balance. The balance is dynamic, undulating between booms and busts, famine, and feast. I fear if we habituate our understanding of birds as being separate from the land then we will never achieve true conservation. To have a system, to maintain a system, other materials are needed.

I firmly believe that this kind of education and understanding can only be achieved through in-situ experience and observation. It is equally fueled by the curiosity and imagination that comes with opening the pages of a book. I have been nourished by many naturalists of the past and present. Reading their words and working to understand their philosophies. This guide is not comprehensive and only touches on a few of the 500 bird species seen in Colorado and a dismally small portion of the plant life. If you are interested in more detailed information on these habitats please see the references and resources sections of this book. It contains a list of all the resources I referenced to write this book in addition to a list of organizations you can contact if you would like to volunteer or find conservation-centered communities.

1. SPRING MIGRATION

Colorado is located within the central flyway, a migration "highway" that birds use to migrate (National Audubon 2015). This makes Colorado a prime location during migration to view a large diversity of species. During spring migration birds are moving quickly. They don't idle at any one location for long periods of time. Males (and in a few species females) are eager to arrive on their breeding grounds to compete for high-quality habitat before females arrive. Migration starts in mid to late April and peaks around the second week of May. It will start slowly with swallows circling intersections, Turkey Vultures floating up the foothills and fewer flocks of ducks and geese at lakes and reservoirs. When May arrives bird life bursts forth with shorebirds visiting our lakesides and flocks of warblers and sparrows moving through the brush and treetops. The high Rockies can still be under several feet of snow in April-May so focus your efforts on low elevation wetlands, wetland adjacent, and riparian hotspots. Areas with a good understory of thick shrubs as well as an overstory of tall cottonwoods, willows, and alders are prime habitats for migrating songbirds like warblers, thrushes, sparrows, etc. This time of year is excellent for rural "migrant traps.". Homesteads with tall stands of trees surrounded by agriculture or prairie (ask permission from property owners before birding on their land!!). Focus your time walking along river walks and lakesides.

Denver Audubon

Rocky Mountain Arsenal

1st Creek at Rocky Mountain Arsenal AND Green Valley Ranch Trail

Highline Canal Trail

Extra Credit:

Tucker Gulch in Golden has regularly produced some of Colorado's most exciting eastern migrants like Hooded and Golden-winged Warbler.

2. FALL MIGRATION

Similar in bird diversity to spring migration but birds spend more time foraging and feeding! Fall migration is my favorite time to bird in Colorado. I love the cold golden mornings, the smell of falling leaves, and difficult IDs. This time of year can pose challenges to even the most seasoned birder. Worn adult birds are molting into their winter plumage, ducks are moving into and out of eclipse plumage, and juvenile birds can have a mix of their first juvenile plumage and the basic adult plumage. That can make for a lot of tricky IDs and exasperated birders! Focus on birding areas with a lot of edge habitat. That could be forest and agriculture, marsh and grassland, riparian and prairie, etc. This will bring many species together including late breeders and migrants from both habitats.

Reservoirs are perfect for this as they often offer overlaps of habitats and increase the diversity and possibility of bird sightings. Reservoirs like Barr Lake State Park are drained in the late summer and provide large mudflats used by shorebirds to fuel up before continuing south. Scan the edges of the shore looking for plovers, yellowlegs, and sandpipers. Look for flocks of sparrows within the thick understory along the banks, and search high in the treetops for migrating warblers.

Recommended Locations

Barr Lake State Park

Rocky Mountain Arsenal

John Martin Reservoir

Pawnee National Grasslands

3. WINTER

Winters in Colorado are cold and dry but they offer an opportunity to practice viewing difficult birds to identify, gulls, and ducks! Viewing both of these families requires patience, warm clothes, and, if you have one, spotting scope. I also recommend joining a local birding group or finding a friend that would enjoy viewing with you. Focus your efforts on large reservoirs with open water. Ducks pair up in the winter months so they are at their peak breeding plumage. While the males are looking sharp and colorful the females are cryptic and can be difficult to ID. Focus on learning the shape of the head, color of the bill, and silhouette of the body.

When learning gulls go with an expert! Frigid days on frozen reservoirs and public dumps are ideal for gull watching. Look to see what was seen in the prior days through ebird and facebook groups and study a bit beforehand. Understand the importance of the bill and leg color, back shading, and eye color. Focus on the overall proportions of the bird in combination with leg, bill, and eye color.

Recommended Locations

Pueblo Reservoir

Chatfield Reservoir

Lake Loveland

Extra Credit: Loveland Dump. Do some research on where and how to park and the best places to view. Visit with someone who has been before.

4. SUMMER

Summer is the time for singing! Summer birding in Colorado is an excellent time to learn some songs. With a large number of breeding species in Colorado, you have the opportunity to perfect your birding by ear! Study before you go. When visiting a new location/ habitat do some research on the birds you'll be able to find there. I recommended learning songs like vocabulary. Choose 2-5 songs and learn them at home. Then go out and try to find them in their appropriate habitat. During the breeding season, all bird species are associated with a specific habitat. Think Yellow Warblers and riparian, or Greater Sage Grouse and Sagebrush. Learning to identify the habitat will help you find birds! The following sections will help you identify and find some of the most prominent and unique habitats in Colorado.

5. SHORT GRASS PRAIRIE

The shortgrass prairie is an overlooked and underappreciated habitat in Colorado. Its golden rolling hills contrast beautifully with the deep blue sky. A wet spring allows for sprawling fields of mallow and primrose. Patient and careful observation might reward you with sightings of Swift Fox, Burrowing Owls, a large variety of unique insects and reptiles. In Colorado, short-grass prairie can be found throughout the eastern plains, usually east of I-25. The most notable areas of short grass prairie are found on the Pawnee Grassland in the northeast portion of the state and the Comanche in the southeast. Short grass prairie is distinguished by low growing grasses with very occasional to absent shrubs. Similar to its alpine cousin, short grass prairie is subjected to extreme weather conditions that have caused specialization within the community. Look for Colorado's state grass Blue Grama Grass as well as Colorado's state bird the Lark Bunting!

Recommended Locations

Rocky Mountain Arsenal

Pawnee National Grassland

Comanche National Grassland

https://en.wikipedia.org/wiki/Lark_bunting#/media/File:Calamospiza_melanocorys_by_Nick_Var
vel.jpg

6. LARK BUNTING

Endemic to the grasslands of North America, and Colorado's state bird, the Lark Bunting is ubiquitous across the short-grass prairie. Males arrive before females on the breeding ground and display by launching into the sky singing complex repeating songs at the peak of their flight and flutter with butterfly-like wingbeats back to the ground. They will utilize both natural prairie and occasionally agriculture areas as breeding habitats but populations decline when areas are over foraged by cattle (Dechant 1999). Lark Buntings winter across the southern United States.

https://en.wikipedia.org/wiki/McCown%27s_longspur#/media/File:Thick-billed_Longspur,_Pakowki_Lake,_Alberta_(cropped).jpg

7. THICK-BILLED LONGSPUR

A denizen of the short grass prairie, the Thick-billed Longspur thrives in areas with sparse grasses, no shrubs, and patches of bare earth. They do well in overgrazed areas but are sensitive to other types of disturbance such as plowing and pesticide application. Look for the diagnostic white "T" in the spread tail as birds fly down dirt country roads. Their range in Northern Colorado lies at the southernmost tip of their breeding distribution with populations in Wyoming, Montana, and Southern Alberta, and Saskatchewan.

Driving slowly along barbed wire fences with windows down, I listened intently for their twittering call. A layer of dust had settled on the interior surfaces of the car and the next layer was circulating the cabin. Had I only left the house on time, always a night owl, I had fought my early alarm. The heat waves warped the horizon obscuring the displaying males and the low afternoon wind reduced aural detection. Just one more stretch I would say prolonging the heat and dehydration. County road after county road I was on my final stretch, headed to the highway home when, out of the deep corner of my eye, I spotted a small gray spot with what seemed like white in the tail. It flew to the top perch of a barbed wire fence and sat, with its neighbor a Horned Lark. Black-capped, and rusty "shouldered," wings out and dropping, legs apart, and mouth open wide. I was not the only one struggling in the summer heat. For several minutes I watched as it looked around, shuffled its feathers, its breast band was matte black and perhaps even slightly mottled. The sun so high and contrasting the bird's mustache stripe could be mistaken for a shadow. It dropped down onto a patch of bare earth below the fence, the whitetail a flag of surrender. I drove home, windows up, air conditioner blasting.

8. LOW ELEVATION RIPARIAN

Riparian habitats are indicated by a water source, a lake, pond, river, stream, etc, and the plant communities associated with them. Riparian habitats can be found at all elevations with plant communities varying in species and morphology. Most riparian is classified by thick sections of willows, tall cottonwoods, alders, and birch. At lower elevations, you'll find shrubs like chokecherries, wild plum, boxelder, and rocky mountain maple. Look for low flowers like spiderwort, milkweeds, lupines, coneflowers, globe mallows, and penstemons. One of the most spacious habitats in Colorado, many avian species utilize it year-round.

Recommended Locations

Denver Audubon

Chatfield State Park

South Platte River-Carson Nature Center

9. YELLOW WARBLER

There is nothing so sweet as the first spring song of the Yellow Warbler. It rings sharp and cordial through the dew-kissed forests on cool spring mornings. Yellow Warbler can be found across Colorado in a variety of elevations. They are one of Colorado's most ubiquitous warblers and Yellow Warblers are riparian specialists (specifically in willows) and decreasing populations can serve as an indicator that something could be affecting the health of the habitat. Listen for their sweet cheerful song coming from treetops on cool spring mornings and listen for the cries of begging fledglings in late summer.

https://pixabay.com/photos/limb-tree-perched-bird-headed-387402/

10. BLACK-HEADED GROSBEAK

This robin sound-alike can be found in a variety of deciduous habitats across the Western United States and breeds throughout Colorado's front range, foothills, and mountains. At lower elevation, they breed in riparian habitats in addition to riparian adjacent scrub. At high elevations, they can be found in deciduous woodlands like aspen groves and along streams and rivers. Both males and females of this species have been recorded singing from the nest but usually sing from the tops or outer branches of trees. Males don't molt into their adult (definitive) plumage until their second year. It is thought that their "female-like" plumage reduces aggression from breeding males.

I remember one particular day early in my birding years I was walking the paths of Red Rocks Amphitheatre. I walked down a paved road where I had a spotting scope set on a nest of a Prairie Falcon's almost-fledged young. I stood at the base of the cliff for almost an hour listening and watching the falcons interact, preen, and sleep. While sitting I listened to and tried to identify the other birds I heard around me. Spotted towhee, Bullock's Oriole, Canyon Wren, White-throated Swift, robin? The robin-like song was long and dynamic in pitch. It didn't have the short trills and subtle harmonics that made American Robins so familiar. I swung the scope to scan the treetops near the song. After minutes of searching, I found him. A Black-headed Grosbeak. Black head shining, orange breast transitioning to yellow, and an enormous seed-crunching bill!

11. HIGH ELEVATION RIPARIAN

Riparian habitats are indicated by a water source, a lake, pond, river, stream, etc, and the plant communities associated with them. High elevation riparian habitats occur above 5,000 feet and are often surrounded by conifer forests of varying types. Look for large thick sections of willows, cottonwoods, aspen, alders, and birch. Furth from the river you'll find chokecherries, raspberries, bog birch, and rocky mountain maple. Depending on elevation look for larkspurs, monkshood, columbines, elephantella, and paintbrush.

Recommended Locations

Staunton State Park

Lake Dillon

Silverthorn, Co

12. CORDILLERAN FLYCATCHER

Breeding primarily in the Rocky Mountains and down into Mexico, the Cordilleran Flycatcher occupies boreal forests composed of pine, spruces, and firs. In Colorado, they can be found above about 4500 feet along small streams and rivers. Cordilleran Flycatchers nest on rocky outcroppings, ledges, root balls of fallen trees, banks of streams, etc. Listen for this bird's sharply ascending whistle/ squeak as you hike through the forest! Cordillera is a geographic term (with Spanish roots) meaning a long chain of uninterrupted mountains. The Cordilleran Flycatcher has year-round and wintering populations in the Rocky Mountain Chain from South Western Canada down to Central Mexico. A flycatcher of the Cordillera.

13. AMERICAN DIPPER

Previously described as the Water Ouzel, the American Dipper is a unique bird and summer resident of streams and rivers of the high Rocky Mountains. Watch as they bounce rhythmically with each step across rocks and streamsides while foraging for aquatic invertebrates. Where the water is high they plunge into the rapids working their way along the streambed searching for their prey. Dippers are adept at moving beneath the ripple currents and will re-emerge meters down or upstream. Which dip was the dipper named for? Its classic dance or its propensity to "dip" beneath the surface. In the winter some dippers move to lower elevation rivers and streams with more open water.

The riverwalk in the town of Morrison is well known (within the birding community) for its dippers. Much like the tourists dining on the patios of riverside restaurants, the dippers perch content on rocks, pulling aquatic insects from the shallows. Occasionally the dipper will plunge into the river, allowing the current to sweep them past submerged hollows and crevices in search of a tasty morsel. Tourists pay for their meals and meander downstream. A highway of concrete carries them to their new destination.

14. SCRUB OAK

Scrub-oak is ubiquitous along Colorado's front range serving as the prelude to the Rocky Mountains. Occurring at 7,000-8,500 it is juxtaposed against other habitats such as short grass prairie, riparian, and ponderosa pine, scrub-oak supports a wide range of plant and animal communities. Many types of plants can be found in the scrub oak community including Gambel's Oak, Mountain Mahogany, junipers, as well as a mix of grasses and wildflowers.

Recommended Locations

Roxborough State Park

Red Rocks Amphitheatre

Morrison, Colorado

15. WOODHOUSE'S SCRUB-JAY

The Woodhouse's Scrub Jay's "Osborn-esque" *eeyyye eyyeee* call can often be heard from both treetops and oak thickets as pairs and small family groups make their way through the habitat. Finding and starting trouble as they go. A year-round resident, this species is common throughout scrubby habitats along Colorado's foothills, sagebrush, pinyon-juniper, and occasionally higher elevation habitats. Woodhouse's Scrub-Jays, as with many other species in the family Corvidae, are known for their caching behavior. Research has shown that jays use often use landmarks to cache and relocate food items (Balda 1989).

16. BUSHTIT

Another year-round resident of Colorado's various scrub and shrub habitats, the Bushtit is a truly delightful species. Bushtits are the only representation of an old-world family containing the "long-tailed tits" and are one of a few species that utilize extra-pair helpers during the breeding season. This behavior varies substantially across its range with up to 37% of nests (in Arizona) having additional birds to help raise the young (Sloane 1992). In the winter months, Bushtits travel in large flocks of up to 40 individuals. On cold winter nights, Bushtits congregate in tight masses inspiring images of John Carpenter-esque conglomerates of tails, eyes, and legs.

Bushtits are surprisingly gregarious. An otherwise quiet and blisteringly hot fall afternoon can suddenly be filled with the trilling of bushtits. They arrive in small numbers at first, a small trill here, a small trill there. Two flit from a low shrub to a short pine tree. They forage efficiently, clinging to the tips of branches poking, and pulling the needles in search of insects. They bounce on. Hardly larger than a cotton ball, you strain your eyes to follow them. Without warning a cascade of trills follows. Bushtits spill from all levels of nearby trees and shrubs, following in a sporadic line behind the original two. Bouncing between shrubs, scampering up cow-shorn willow branches, and slipping off the tips of nodding flower heads. The deeper into the foliage you look the more there seems to be. Like an amoeba, they move in an undulating fashion through the scrublands. Like a single organism, they reach out to encompass a new shrub. Until they are suddenly gone.

17. SAGEBRUSH SHRUB

Located from about 7,000 to 10,000 feet elevation, sagebrush shrub habitat is an extensive habitat across the western and southwestern states. Including Colorado, Wyoming, Utah, Idaho, Nevada, Montana, and Oregon, sagebrush landscapes evoke images of the wild west, cowboys, vast open spaces, and big blue skies. It is dominated by a plethora of large shrub species including several species of sagebrush, rabbitbrush, and bitterbrush. While it can feel like a wasteland it is truly a desert paradise. Hot dry evenings give way to cool nights and skies filled with booming nighthawks. Large packs of coyotes fill the night air with yips and howls and strutting sage grouse begin their dance well before the rise of the sun. Birds of the great sagebrush steppe include Sage Thrashers, Common Nighthawk, Common Raven, and Brewer's Sparrow.

Recommended Locations

Walden

Gunnison

https://en.wikipedia.org/wiki/Gunnison_grouse#/media/File:Centrocercus_minimus.jpg

18. GUNNISON SAGE-GROUSE

Colorado's second of two endemic species, the Gunnison Sage-Grouse's range extends around the town of Gunnison, Co with some small populations further west and one in Utah. Gunnison Sage-Grouse is distinguished by its smaller size, more prominent filoplumes behind the head, and more white in the tail than their "Greater" cousin. Pressures from agriculture, irrigation projects, livestock, and housing developments have caused reductions in their historic range (Young 2000). Disturbance at nest and breeding sites has also caused a decrease in reproductive success. Conservation efforts including habitat restoration, hunting regulations, population transplanting, and predator control have all been implemented in an attempt to increase populations.

Two in the morning arrived as quickly as one would expect. I consumed my breakfast with great reservations and donned several layers of clothing. I met a friend at a poorly lit parking lot. We combine our gear and set off on our drive promising our bodies sleep when we arrive. Two hours later we parked behind a long line of other vehicles sitting dark and silent. It's March in Gunnison, Colorado. Winter hasn't left the mountains and snowdrifts still stand taller than me. Windows wide open and frigid air shaking our bodies we can hear a distant Sage Thrasher singing a melodic and occasionally repeating song. We strain our ears for the classic booming of the grouse. Silence. We chat quietly, looking at others hoping to see binoculars spring up. A sign they have spotted the target. Hours pass and the sun crests the eastern Rockies. The small valley is washed in golden-red light. Large Sage Brushes stand tall, their branch tips swaying. As we realize the birds we've come to see aren't here we begin mingling with birders in other cars. One car saw a grouse fly over the crest of the hill 45 min ago, we had missed it in our discussion. While we missed our target species we found ourselves in a beautiful landscape. Mountain peaks towered around us and the silvery-blue sagebrush contrasted strongly with the golden sunrise. A birdless morning is still beautiful.

19. SAGEBRUSH SPARROW

The Sagebrush Sparrow is one of my favorite sparrows with its silvery-sage head contrasting strongly with a white supralore, malar, throat, and bold eyering. Easily overlooked, Sagebrush Sparrows often forage for seeds and insects on the ground, running from shrub rather than flying. Sagebrush Sparrows breed on Colorado's western sagebrush slopes and are occasionally but regularly seen in low numbers on the front range during migration. As their name suggests they are closely associated with sagebrush habitats preferring areas with large patchy shrubs (Wiens 1981). They spend their winters in the southwestern United States and northern Mexico.

20. PINYON-JUNIPER

Pinyon-Juniper habitat is common throughout the western slopes of Colorado as well as the east slope south of Colorado Springs. Habitat is most developed at 5,000-7,000 feet and is designated by evenly spaced Pinyon Pine and mixed juniper woodlands with density increasing with elevation and moisture availability. Cold tolerant pines may dominate higher elevation PJ habitat while drought-tolerant junipers dominate lower elevation areas. The understory is composed of a mix of shrubs including Three-leaf Sumac, Mountain Mahogany, Rabbitbrush, and varying sagebrushes depending on geographic region. Many species within these forest types are specialists on pinyon pine seeds including Scrub and Pinyon Jays.

Recommended Locations

Walsenburg, Co

Hotchkiss, Co

Paonia, Co

https://en.wikipedia.org/wiki/Pinyon_jay#/media/File:Gymnorhinus_cyanocephalus1.jpg

21. PINYON JAY

Pinyon Jays are gregarious birds that travel in well-organized and highly social groups. They are some of the earliest breeding birds in the United States because of their ability to rely on cached foods to feed young. Their close association with pinyon pines causes large interruptions in populations and distribution when cone crops fail within their typical range. Pinyon Jays nest communally with yearling males attending their younger siblings. Listen for their cackling calls as they fly between mesa tops.

In 2016 I was walking through an apple orchard on Colorado's western slope. The trees were planted in dense rows and I could not see over them but they created a long pathway to the edge of the hillside. At the base of the hillside, I heard a single cackle as the silhouette of a dark bird flew over my head, tail protruding like the bristles on the broomstick. It perched gently atop a pine tree, its long wings flicked into place. It appeared gray and drab, cackling again it pulled a seed from a cone at its feet. I watched hoping she would cache the seed, but she was wary. She examined me but did not move. Another bird appeared, below, cackling and pulling seeds from cones. And another, hanging off the end of a branch. And yet another scratching through the duff on the forest floor. And suddenly ten birds stood around the one, jumping, scratching, pulling, all cackling. Who were they laughing at? The first bird had disappeared. I did not see her go. I was taken in by the chaos of the flock. Perhaps she had conjured them. One by one, a mess of replicants repeating her movements moment by moment. When I had been thoroughly enchanted by her spell she fled, to cache her treasure.

https://en.wikipedia.org/wiki/Juniper_titmouse#/media/File:Juniper_Titmouse2.jpg

22. JUNIPER TITMOUSE

A dispersed and uncommon species in continuous Pinyon-Juniper woodlands, the Juniper Titmouse is a year-round resident in Colorado. They are distributed across the west slope, down along the southern border, and uncommon through the shrubs of southeastern Colorado. They remain in pairs during the breeding and winter season and do not join mixed nomadic flocks. Generally, Juniper Titmouse consumes pinyon pine seeds and insects they glean along branches and pine needles. More research is needed to understand the diversity of the Juniper Titmouse's diet as well as many other characteristics about its life.

23. HIGH DESERT/ SEMI DESERT SHRUBLAND

Occurring below 7,500 and designated by high brushy plateaus and riparian-bottomed canyons the high desert is one of Colorado's most breathtaking habitats. This habitat can be found mostly on the west slope, centering around Grand Junction, west to Utah, and south to New Mexico. Isolated semi-desert shrub can be found near Canyon City to Walsenburg. Plant diversity is lower than other habitats in Colorado and many of its plant and animal communities are unique to the high desert. Look for miles of sagebrush, greasewood, and saltbush interrupted with deep red sandstone, white gypsum, and shale geological formations.

Recommended Locations

Canyons of the Ancients

24. LUCY'S WARBLER

The smallest warbler in the United States, the Lucy's Warbler, inhabits riparian mesquite canyon corridors of South West United States and North Western Mexico. Present in a very small handful of locations on Colorado's southwest slope this warbler can be difficult to find. The males arrive earlier than many other warbler species singing from the treetops by late March. They nest in heavily concealed tree cavities, beneath pieces of loose bark, in old woodpecker cavities, or roots along river banks (Harrison 1979). They are threatened by the loss of riparian habitat.

25. BLACK-THROATED SPARROW

A summer resident in Colorado, the Black-throated Sparrow can be found on our western slopes and some locations on the Comanche National Grassland in our southeast plains. Black-throated Sparrows prefer open shrubland with evenly spaced vegetation including sagebrush, cholla, yucca, and prickly pear. Black-throated Sparrows are short-distance migrants only going as far as the southern United States and Mexico. They feed on seeds and insects working their way around the base of and through low shrubs. During the breeding season, I often hear their small light "chip" emanating from low shrubs. Males will sit tall in shrubs to sing, sometimes chasing nearby or encroaching males out of their territory.

Dark clouds gathered overhead and distant ripples of thunder tumbled down the canyon. I walked on a wide gravel road, red dust billowing at my feet. On either side of the road shallow slopes lead to steep red cliff faces. A small flock of swifts chittered loudly and dove low along the slopeside. I crossed a dry wash as I felt the first raindrop. A small *"plink"* from a pair of shrubs accompanied it. Another *"plink"* across the road. A rush of movement darted across the road and between the shrubs ending atop the larger one. Two sparrows sat tall and adjacent to one another. The first one sang, its song beginning with two short notes then slid into a serrated buzz. Midsong the second bird begins to sing. They overlap and interrupt each other for less than 15 seconds before one dives, somehow disappearing within the sparse vegetation. The remaining bird continues to sing, uninterrupted, for another 30 or so seconds before also descending into the brush. Their spat now over the quiet *"plinks"* continue moving gently through the brush.

26. PONDEROSA PINE

Ascending in elevation from scrub oak (5,600-9,000ft) is the Ponderosa Pine habitat. Ponderosa Pines are very large pine trees with a loose reddish light brown bark broken by larger dark crevices. Some ponderosas can be very large standing over 100 feet tall and have immense trunks! Ponderosa Pine forests are generally very open forests with an understory of sparse shrubs, kinikinik, grasses, and sparse wildflowers including penstemons and pasque flowers! Walk up and smell the bark to experience a strong, sweet, butterscotchy scent. Ponderosa Pine habitat is home to many species of birds including kinglets, nuthatches, crossbills, raptors, turkeys, and more! Keep an eye out for Ponderosa Pine's star mammal the Abert's Squirrel. A medium-sized grey to black squirrel with long tufted ears.

Recommended Locations

Genesee Mountain Park

Lory State Park

Mount Falcon

https://en.wikipedia.org/wiki/Williamson%27s_sapsucker#/media/File:Williamson's_Sapsucker_-_Sisters_-_Oregon_S4E1518_(19038668100).jpg

27. WILLIAMSON'S SAPSUCKER

Across their range in the Rocky and Sierra Nevada Mountain Ranges, William Sapsuckers are a species residing in high elevation coniferous forests. In Colorado, they occupy areas within and between Ponderosa Pine and Douglas Fir forests choosing nesting locations adjacent to open ponderosa pine woodlands (Crockett 1975). Williamson's Sapsuckers occur in Colorado's Rocky Mountains during the breeding season (May-August) and migrate to the southern rocky mountains and Mexico for the winter (Howell 1995, American Ornithologists Union 1983). Williamson's Sapsuckers are seasonally monogamous and occasionally maintain the same pair bond for multiple seasons (Crockett). Like their name suggests this species feeds exclusively on conifer sap during the pre-nesting period and during the breeding season they are almost completely dependent on ants (Beal 1911). Adults forage for ants on tree trunks and branches as the ants move up and down tending to aphids (Smith 1982).

28. BROWN CREEPER

Brown Creepers have delighted me as long as I've been birding. Their likeness to tree bark is so remarkable that only the sharpest eye can spot them. Their torpedo-like dive might catch your eye as they move from tree-top to trunk bottom and their delightful single trilled call sounds as if they are singing out "trees" in excitement. Common across the United States, in Colorado, Brown Creepers breed in high elevation conifer forests beneath large loose pieces of bark on the trunks of dead and dying trees. In the winter months, they can often be found traveling within mixed flocks of chickadees and kinglets. Listen for a high-pitched single "trill" or "trees" as they forage on trunks spiraling from the bottom to the top of the tree!

Brown Creepers are famously cryptic. Their variegated bark-like plumage is difficult to see at a distance so one must rely on movement or the ability to hear their single high-pitched trill. I remember one particular sighting while I was in college in Fort Collins. I was sitting at the kitchen table looking out the glass door that faced into the back alley. Trash bins lay in disarray between the apartments and a perpetually oil-slicked pothole puddle was a favorite water source for the local robins. In this alleyway was a tall Russian Elm. Struggling to survive amongst the concrete. As I ate my breakfast a small brown bird flew and landed at the base of the tree working its way quickly and diligently to the first large branch. It circled the trunk and lower largest branches several times before flitting off to a more arborous neighborhood. I felt as if I had just witnessed "stopover" habitat in miniature. A failing Russian Elm in a tiny polluted parking lot was not an ideal habitat. But it did serve as a stopover between more ideal habitats. Birds will utilize all habitats if needed and it is so easy to provide higher quality urban habitats by simply planting wisely.

29. DOUGLAS FIR

Douglas Fir is situated with lodgepole pine from 6,000-95,000 just above Ponderosa Pine on an elevational gradient. Dominated by my favorite tree the Douglas Fir (*Pseudotsuga menziesii*). One of the first Latin names I ever learned, and one that runs off the tongue so smoothly sood-oh-soogah men-zee-zee-eye. The pine cones of this species are easily identified by small bracts protruding from each scale of the cone. These bracts look a bit like (if we use our imagination) a tiny mouse hiding beneath the scales, only its little feet and tail sticking out. In addition to Douglas Fir, lodgepole, limber, or ponderosa pine can also be present. The understory in Douglas Fir communities is composed of shrubs like Nine-bark, wild raspberry, wild rose, and rocky mountain maple. Look for wildflowers like the Fairy Slipper Orchid and Heart-leaf Arnica throughout June and into early July. Birds of Douglas Fir forest include Red Crossbill, Cassin's Finch, and Steller's Jay (Benedict 2008).

Recommended Locations

Staunton State Park

30. RUBY-CROWNED KINGLET

In Colorado, the Ruby-crowned Kinglet breeds, in sometimes high densities, throughout the mid-high elevation conifer forests. During migration, they can be found across the front range and prairie traveling with groups of chickadees and warblers. Their song is loud, melodic, and gregarious and is the easiest way to detect them during the breeding season. Listen for their small *"ch-ch"* alarm/contact call as they move about the outer branches of trees and shrubs. Despite their diminutive size kinglets are known to have nests with up to 12 eggs! The Ruby-crowned Kinglet is comparative in morphology to the Golden-crowned Kinglet, but some genetic evidence does not support a close relation (Packert 2003).

The song of the Ruby-crowned Kinglet sticks in my mind like a stubborn price sticker on a grocery store candle. On many hot June mornings, I have hiked through Colorado's Rocky Mountains with kinglets singing from every nook and cranny. Crests pulsating they stand their ground against other males pressing into their territory. Singing and counter singing until every tree drips with melody. The sticker may be gone but the residue remains. I fell asleep those nights with the kinglet's song stuck onto my subconscious.

31. RED-BREASTED NUTHATCH

The smart black cap and dark striking eye-line of the Red-breasted Nuthatch make it one of my favorite boreal birds. The Red-breasted Nuthatch breeds across the boreal forests of North America and throughout Colorado's Rocky Mountains. They can be found during migration and the winter months throughout the front range and well onto the plains during irruption years caused by low food quantity or quality in their breeding habitat. They are common in mixed flocks of chickadees, kinglets, and creepers in the winter. Its toy-trumpet call precedes it and it's coming entourage.

32. LODGEPOLE PINE

7500-10,000 ft Lodgepole Pine forests are identified by their seemingly "empty" forest structures. Trees are distributed seemingly randomly across the needle-matted forest floor. Only prostrate plants like kinikinik and juniper cover the ground. Areas of bare dirt and lichen-covered rocks are common. Lodgepole pine forests are lower in diversity than other neighboring forest types but don't let that fool you. Lodgepole pines are resilient trees that many species utilize and rely on. Lodgepole is often the first tree to spring forth from fire or insect plagued areas beginning a new era of succession. Pine Squirrels (or Chickarees), a pine specialist, utilize cones as food and trees as cover. In turn, the squirrel middens provide food and habitat for the Red-backed Vole, another lodgepole/ spruce specialist species. Lodgepole pine cones are serotinous, which means they require fire to open and drop their seeds. This makes lodgepole pines dependent on wildfires for reproduction and generational succession (Benedict 2008).

Recommended Locations

Allen's Park

Lory State Park

State Forest State Park

Staunton State Park

33. DARK-EYED JUNCO

Dark-eyed Juncos are a highly variable sparrow consisting of five informal "groups." Dark-eyed Juncos breed across the Western and North Western and North Eastern United States, Canada, and Alaska. In Colorado, the "Grey-headed" group breeds in high elevation coniferous forests including Ponderosa and Lodgepole forests. Juncos often nest on the ground under rocky outcroppings, fallen logs, ferns, tree trunks, and occasionally on elevated surfaces like fences, vines, and horizontal branches (Peck 1998). In the winter all five groups can be found along the foothills and front range areas at feeders and habitats with low bushes and grass. This is a great time to study the variation between and within the species!

In September hot summer afternoons are followed by cold fall nights and crisp clear mornings. Geese congregate in larger and larger numbers, their undulating flights stretch across Denver as they spiral down to their evening roost. The last song of a Yellow Warbler was months before and Snowy Tree Crickets fiddle from wilting plants. In October when the leaves are ablaze and each night comes with the threat of snow; the Dark-eyed Junco finally arrives. In small flocks, they forage among low leafless shrubs on seeds, dried berries, and perhaps a hidden frozen insect. At the first drop of a snowflake, they cover the ground of bird feeding stations. Almost fully rounded they bounce along leaving small light footprints wherever they go. Many different variations make up Colorado's wintering junco population; their pastel colors blend beautifully with Colorado's winter landscape. Soft pink sides and dark backs match the bare mauve branches and dark brown soils.

34. RED CROSSBILL

In Colorado, crossbills can be found in high elevation conifer forests including lodgepole, douglas fir, and spruce/fir. Red Crossbills are aptly named as the top of the bill crosses over the bottom, this allows birds to pry open cones and consume the seeds inside. Because of this adaptation, different populations of Red Crossbills have begun to specialize on single species of tree. Subtle morphological (structural differences) differences in the bill allow birds to become highly specialized in feeding on a single species of cone (Benkeman 1993). These slightly differing bill morphologies also create slight differences in the calls of the crossbills. This makes it possible for birdwatchers to identify which Crossbills we are hearing and what type of tree they feed on.

35. SUBALPINE FIR

Starting at about 10,000 feet elevation, Subalpine Fir is dominated by, obviously, Subalpine fir and also Engelmann Spruce. Its understory is thicker and wetter than lodgepole and ponderosa habitats with rotting fallen trees, mats of Vaccinium, shrubs like birch, cinquefoil, and currants. Mosses, lichens, and a variety of forbs and grasses fill out areas between fallen trees and shrubs. Keep an eye out for arnica, chiming bells, larkspur, monkshood, and other flowers. Listen and look for thrushes, crossbills, nutcrackers, nuthatches, and more! The complexity and density of plant life make this habitat one of my favorite habitats.

Recommended Locations

Guanella Pass (Various hiking trails)

Golden Gate State Park

Red Feather Lakes

36. HERMIT THRUSH

From my first encounter, the ethereal song of the Hermit Thrush has been a siren calling me to the high mountains. Hermit Thrushes (and many other thrush/ bird species) have unique vocal structures that allow them to sing multiple notes at a single time. This allows them to create small harmonies within their song. The Hermit Thrush is one of the most widespread thrushes in North America nesting in a wide variety of forested habitats across the United States, Canada, and Mexico. In Colorado, they occupy Douglas and Subalpine Fir habitats.

I stood surrounded by towering silver-green Subalpine Fir. A maze of fallen trees lies scattered across the forest floor, each one home to an ecosystem of brilliant green mosses, pastel lichens, and a variety of unique insect life. Spring runoff meandered across the path and descended deep into layers of decaying wood joining other rivulets to create trickling streams. Upon what ground I could see were thick mats of flowering plants. Arnica, fireweed, blueberry, Solomon's seal, and occasional bluebells flanked the narrow path on both sides before it dropped to precarious slopes. A familiar sound began to creep into the forest. I continued walking, the sound moving through the understory as if I were to give chase. The song became clear, the harmonies are crisp and hollow. It fell upon the forest floor, a tributary of the melting runoff. The sound was not loud but washed through the crevices of the forest floor reaching life in even the darkest places. As I passed, the liquid song seemed to part, echoing all around me as I entered into the eye of the storm and then waning as we moved our separate ways into the dark forest floor.

https://en.wikipedia.org/wiki/Golden-
crowned_kinglet#/media/File:Golden_crowned_kinglet_6122.jpg

37. GOLDEN-CROWNED KINGLET

Its body is the size of a half-dollar coin, weighing as little as two nickels, its striking golden-yellow crown reminds those of its true hierarchy. The Golden-crowned Kinglet's crown is gaudy yellow/orange, pulsating, rising, and falling during interactions with rivaling neighbors (Morse 1970). Golden-crowned Kinglets live and breed in the boreal forests of North America. In Colorado, they occupy higher elevation forests singing and moving about the tallest trees. These tiny kings live big lives often raising multiple clutches a season, sometimes starting its second clutch before the first has even fledged

(Galati 1991). Listen for their high-pitched calls and songs as you hike through this beautiful habitat.

38. ALPINE TUNDRA

Impacted by the short growing seasons, strong winds, and varying rainfall, the alpine tundra is composed of a variety of microhabitats. Tundras can be microcosms of diversity with wetlands, snowfields, meadows, and grasslands all supporting forbes, grasses, lichens, and mosses. In addition to plant life, biotic soil structures support populations of funguses, mosses, lichens, and bacteria. When hiking in the tundra, stay on the trail. Biotic soils are very delicate and take many years to recover from trampling. While hiking, try to spot wildflowers like Old Man of the Mountain, large alpine sunflowers, a variety of grasses, sedges, and shrubs like birch and cinquefoil. Birdlife in the tundra is surprisingly abundant with Ptarmigan, pipits, rosy-finches, horned larks, and even some populations of Brewer's Sparrow!

Recommended Locations

Guanella Pass

Mount Evans

Medicine Bow Curve Trail Ridge Road Rocky Mountain National Park

https://en.wikipedia.org/wiki/Brown-capped_rosy_finch#/media/File:Brown-capped_rosy_finch.jpg

39. BROWN-CAPPED ROSY-FINCH

There are three species of rosy finch in the United States with Brown-capped being the only one that breeds in Colorado. One of Colorado's two (mostly) endemic species. Its range is restricted to the Colorado Rocky Mountains and a few locations in Northern New Mexico. Brown-capped Rosy-Finches breed in the boulder fields above treeline (11,000-14,000ft) often foraging on snowfields and glaciers for frozen insects and seeds. A winter snowstorm can bring all three species of Rosy-finches to neighborhood bird feeders located in the foothills and mountains along with the front range.

It was later winter and the weather report called for significant snow across the front range. Having seen this report I had begged my mother to take me to the amphitheater where the finches had been seen. We arrived to frigid temperatures and thick fluffy snowflakes falling fast and hard. They stuck to every surface building up miniature drifts along wall faces and power lines. We stood on the upper deck behind the trading post watching and waiting. Juncos were here, pink-sided, slate-colored, and more. White-crowned Sparrows sang occasionally from the nearby shrubs, and Western Scrub-Jays jeered from tall pines. A small flock of birds came in from a distant rock face. They swerved and landed at the feeding station. They decorated every surface, their soft brown and pink plumage blended so naturally into the environment. Rosy-finches on the ground, on the hopper feeder, the rocks behind the feeders had a coating of finches. The small crowd there to see them was delighted. They oohed and awed as groups of finches came and went. And suddenly they were gone. All of them. They took off flying up the face of the rocks perhaps to perch from the secret hideaway from which they originally came.

https://en.wikipedia.org/wiki/Buff-bellied_pipit#/media/File:Anthus_rubescens_-Harney_County,_Oregon,_USA-8.jpg

40. AMERICAN PIPIT

Throughout its global range, the American Pipit breeds in high arctic areas above treeline nesting on the ground, eroded banks, and wet and dry meadows. Almost always under overhanging vegetation.

Nest sitting is done exclusively by the female but the young are fed by both adults. Often seen on snowfields, their diet consists of terrestrial and aquatic invertebrates and seeds. During the breeding season watch for American Pipits above treeline as they lark, singing their song as they arc across the tundra only to land in exactly the spot they initially arose. American Pipits can also be seen in large numbers foraging on mudflats, shorelines, and seasonal playas across the front range of Colorado during spring and fall migration.

41. OPEN WATER RESERVOIR

While the majority of reservoirs across Colorado are not "native habitats" but man-made ones, the birdlife can still be quite diverse. Often adjacent to open shoreline, agriculture, prairies, rivers, wetlands, or small deltas these reservoirs can be a migrant trap of sorts attracting a wide variety of waterfowl, shorebirds, and passerines to their shores to breed and migrate. A number of unique species use these reservoirs to reproduce including Black Terns, Piping Plovers, Snowy Plovers, and Least Terns. All of these species are considered threatened or endangered. If you plan to look for them, bring a spotting scope and expect beach closures. Respect all closures as well as the bird's personal space.

Recommended Locations

Chatfield State Park

Cherry Creek State Park

Barr Lake State Park

John Martin Reservoir

https://pixabay.com/photos/piping-plover-endangered-beach-bird-3615164/

42. PIPING PLOVER

A very uncommon breeder in Colorado and equally uncommon migrant, the Piping Plover is a phantom of the shoreline. Their wavering "peeweeep" call can be heard as they fly over the flats. Watch from a distance as they scurry up and down the beach in search of insects. Stakeout dead fish or other carcasses as chicks often feed on insects attracted to the carcasses. The small handful of breeding areas in Colorado are heavily monitored for predation, trespassing, and other threats to these breeding birds. Always respect beach closures!

The tide was at its lowest and a mile or more of flats lay bared. Through the mist, I could scarcely make out the geography ahead. Groups of shorebirds moved in purposeful directions -bill to the ground- foraging as they went. A distant godwit stands tall, watching me as I move. It steps slowly, considers foraging then merely stops to watch me pass. As I pass I heard a long sad peeeeweeeep. To my right, the plover lands touching the ground at a run. The gray sand, gray fog, and gray sky merge together creating a vacuum. An absence. The plover scampers into view. Gray on gray on gray. Its black eye watches me intensely. It calls again and pulls something from the mud. Running along parallel to me as I walk. It is just me and this plover. The only two things I can perceive for miles. The ground I walk on exists but beyond me the land is empty, the sky is empty, and they are joined in the center by a thin reflection of a shorebird standing small and round.

https://en.wikipedia.org/wiki/Least_tern#/media/File:Least_Tern_(Sternula_antillarum)_RWD1.jpg

43. LEAST TERN

Another uncommon migrant and breeder on Colorado's prairie reservoirs is the Least Tern. The world's smallest species of tern, it resembles a swift or a swallow in flight. They nest in colonies on open flats and beaches and feed on small nearshore fish, crustaceans, and arthropods. Because its habitat overlaps so heavily with human-favored vacationing areas it has been greatly reduced and is threatened by dogs, off-road vehicles, and general beach activities.

44. CANYON COUNTRY

Colorado has ample canyon country throughout the state and especially along the front range where the Morrison layer is uplifted and exposed giving us locations such as Red Rocks Amphitheatre, Roxborough State Park, and Garden of Gods. In the southeast portion of the state vast flat prairies are broken by deep canyons and to the west, Black Canyon of the Gunnison fractures the mountains as if they are composed of butter. Surrounding habitats, plant communities, and elevations can vary depending on the location; there are a few species that specialize in the microhabitats provided in the vertical cliff faces themselves including Rock Wrens, Canyon Wrens, and swifts.

Recommended Locations

Red Rocks Amphitheatre

Roxborough State Park

Mesa Verde

45. CANYON WREN

There is nothing so emblematic of canyon country as the song of a Canyon Wren. Its song starts as a slow whistle ascending slightly in pitch before speeding up and descending by several notes, giving the impression that the bird is tumbling down the cliff face. Canyon Wrens can be found throughout Colorado where ever canyons or cliff faces exist. Listen for the loud and clear song and watch for them as they forage up and down the cliff face clinging with their long toes to the vertical walls. Their stunning reddish hues and fine spots camouflage them against the Morrison layer's red dusty sandstone. The Canyon Wren's very long slender bill is evolved to pull insects from the thinnest rock crevices.

https://en.wikipedia.org/wiki/White-throated_swift#/media/File:White-throated_Swift_(Aeronautes_saxatalis)_in_flight.jpg

46. WHITE-THROATED SWIFT

One of my favorite species, the exhilarating acrobatics of the White-throated Swift are entertaining and heart-stopping! Found throughout the interior west the White-throated Swift is specifically found near canyons and cliffs as they nest with the crevices and cracks across the cliff face. Swifts, aptly described as cigars with wings, are a highly specialized family. Morphologically similar to swallows, the similarities arose independently as the families are not closely related. Listen for the descending scratching calls of swifts as they plummet from immense heights barely pulling up before striking the ground.

I was hiking on an expansive cattle ranch in Southeast Colorado at the bottom of a steep canyon. The riverbed was dry and lined with lush green foliage. Willows, cottonwoods, and alder stood thick along the shore. I was early in my bird education and the songs slurred together, House Wrens perhaps sang from a nearby thicket, maybe a Blue Grosbeak stood tall along a meadow edge. Orioles must have been chattering and chasing one another from treetop to treetop. The bird I do remember, clearly and vividly is the White-throated Swift. They chattered loudly, interrupting the otherwise peaceful spring morning. Small groups chased one another, diving and swinging sharply around canyon corners. We had stopped to investigate the home of a tarantula when two swifts, entangled, plummeted to the ground before us arguing as they went. Just before they struck the earth they parted and flew gracefully off and up into the blue.

47. BACKYARD/ URBAN

Backyards and other urban areas can be a great place to see a variety of birds! Neighborhoods that back up to green spaces or older neighborhoods with tall trees are best for birding but any neighborhood has birds. Try one of the options below to attract birds to your yard.

48. BIRD FEEDERS

Food. Even within seed-eating birds, there is diet variation. Try different types and seeds and different types of feeders based on what you have or what you want to attract. Goldfinches, and House both love sunflower and thistle seeds. Thistle sock feeders are very popular with finches and are a low-cost option! On the other hand, sunflower seeds attract finches but also a wide variety of other birds like chickadees, woodpeckers, and blackbirds. Some folks find large flocks of blackbirds unfavorable because of their ability to eat large quantities of seed in such short times. Experiment and see what lives in your area!

H2O! One of the best ways to attract birds to your yard is to add water. This can be as easy as setting up a birdbath to building a small pond or fountain. Bird feeders only cater to those species of birds that feed on seeds but all birds need water! Adding a water feature to your yard will attract a larger variety of species than a feeder will. Make sure you are able to maintain a clean birdbath or pond. This helps reduce disease and mosquitoes populations.

Gardening. Gardening is the best way to attract birds to your yard. Contact a garden center or local Audubon chapter to find a list of native plants in your area. Try to choose plants of all different "levels." You want a mix of trees, shrubs, wildflowers, and even grasses. While we humans are at constant odds with the insects in our gardens, attracting them is good for birds! So DON'T SPRAY! Attracting birds means attracting bugs. Native plants will bring in a larger variety of birds than any feeder ever will.

49. WHAT TO PLANT

In Colorado focus on layering your garden with shrubs, wildflowers, and grasses. Chokecherry, wild plum, rabbitbrush, saltbush, sage brushes, and three-leaf sumac are all native and favorites of birds. All of these plants produce seeds in the summer and fall that birds will utilize throughout the fall and winter months. Native wildflowers will support insects and birds as well as bringing color and life to your garden. Plants like sunflower, columbine, larkspur, prairie smoke, and pasque flower all bloom at different times of the year. Your garden will have color all summer and seeds and insects will provide birds with lots of food and cover. There are a number of beautiful native grasses that serve as wonderful accents to any garden. Our state grass, the Blue Gramma, is a delightful species growing between 12-16 inches tall with delicate "eyelash" shaped seed heads. Big bluestem is a beautiful and regal species that grows 6-7 feet tall and looks stunning along a path or garden edge. All of these species are native and when combined strategically will provide food and cover for birds year-round!

OTHER HELPFUL RESOURCES

Denver Audubon-https://denveraudubon.org/

Denver Field Ornithologist-https://dfobirds.org/

Colorado Field Ornithologist-https://cobirds.org/

The Cornell Lab of Ornithology-https://www.birds.cornell.edu/

eBird-https://ebird.org/home An online database of bird observations providing scientists, researchers, and amateur naturalists with real-time data about bird distribution and abundance.

Birds of the World-https://birdsoftheworld.org/bow/home A website with species information for all birds in the United States.

XenoCanto-https://www.xeno-canto.org/ An excellent website for searching and downloading bird songs and calls. Users can contribute to the database as well.

Works Cited

American Ornithologists' Union (1983). Check-list of North American Birds. Edition 6. American Ornithologists' Union, Lawrence, KS, USA.https://www.biodiversitylibrary.org/page/34735248

Balda, R. P., and A. C. Kamil (1989). A comparative study of cache recovery by three corvid species. Animal Behaviour 38:486–495.

Beal, F. E. L. (1911). Food of the woodpeckers of the United States. U.S. Department of Agriculture, Biological Survey Bulletin 37.

Benedict, Audrey D., and Audrey D. Benedict. *The Naturalist's Guide to the SOUTHERN Rockies: Colorado, SOUTHERN Wyoming, and Northern New Mexico*. Fulcrum Pub., 2008.

Benkman, C. W. (1993a). Adaptation to single resources and the evolution of crossbill (Loxia) diversity. Ecological Monographs 63:305–325.https://doi.org/10.2307/2937103

Benkman, C. W. (1990). Foraging rates and the timing of crossbill reproduction. Auk 107:376-386.

Crockett, A. B. and H. H. Hadow. (1975). Nest site selection by Williamson's and Red-naped sapsuckers. Condor 77:365-368.

Crockett, A. B. (1975a). Ecology and behavior of the Williamson's Sapsucker in Colorado. Phd Thesis, Univ. of Colorado, Boulder.

Dechant, J. A., M. L. Sondreal, D. H. Johnson, L. D. Igl and C. M. Goldade. (1999b). Effects of management practices on grassland birds: Lark Bunting. Jamestown, ND: Northern Prairie Wildl. Res. Center.

Galati, B. (1991). Golden-crowned Kinglets: treetop nesters of the north woods. Ames: Univ. Iowa Press.

Harrison, H. H. (1979). A Field Guide to Western Birds' Nests. Houghton Mifflin Company, Boston, MA, USA.

Howell, S. N. G., and S. Webb (1995). A Guide to the Birds of Mexico and Northern Central America. Oxford University Press, New York, NY, USA.

Morse, D. H. (1970). Ecological aspects of some mixed species foraging flocks of birds. Ecological Monographs 40:119–168.

Päckert, M., J. Martens, J. Kosuch, A. A. Nazarenko and M. Veith. (2003). Phylogenetic signal in the song of crests and kinglets (Aves: Regulus). Evolution 57 (3):616-629.

Peck, G. K. (1998). Ontario birds. J. Ontario Field Nat. 16:11

Sloane, S. A. (1992). Supernumeraries at Bushtit (Psaltriparus minimus) nests: incidence, origins, and proximate causes. Phd Thesis, Univ. of Michigan, Ann Arbor.

Smith, K. G. (1982d). On habitat selection of Williamson's and "Red-naped" Yellow-bellied Sapsuckers. Southwestern Naturalist 27:464-466.

Wiens, J. A. and J. T. Rotenberry. (1981b). Habitat associations and community structure of birds in shrubsteppe environments. Ecological Monographs 5:21-41.

Young, J. R., C. E. Braun, S. J. Oyler-McCance, J. W. Hupp and T. W. Quinn. (2000). A new species of Sage-Grouse (Phasianidae: Centrocercus) from southwestern Colorado. Wilson Bulletin 112 (4):445-453

READ OTHER
50 THINGS TO KNOW ABOUT BIRDS IN THE UNITED STATES BOOKS

50 Things to Know

Stay up to date with new releases on Amazon:

https://amzn.to/2VPNGr7

CZYKPublishing.com

50 Things to Know

We'd love to hear what you think about our content! Please leave your honest review of this book on Amazon and Goodreads. We appreciate your positive and constructive feedback. Thank you.